WORDS IN EDGEWAYS

By
Kenneth Clelland

Four Dramatic Monologues

Including

Articles of Faith part 1: His Wonders to Perform...........7
Articles of Faith part 2: A Blaze of Glory......................17
Splitting Hairs..27
Impure as the Driven......................................41
A Delicate Balance (Pontius Pilate)...............59

© 2016 by Kenneth Clelland

The right Tim Jenkins as Kenneth Clelland to be identified as the Author of the Work has been asserted by him in accordance with the Copyright, Design and Patents Act 1988.

All rights whatsoever in these monologues are strictly reserved and application for permission to perform or reproduce in any form, print, stage, film etc., all or part of any of these monologues, must be made in advance, before rehearsals begin to:

Fire Circle Publishing, 9a Craddock's Parade,
Ashtead, Surrey KT21 1QL

All characters in this publication and any resemblance to real persons living or dead is purely coincidental

ISBN: 978-0-9930313-3-5

Cover Design and text lay out by Tim Jenkins using Serif PagePlus and DrawPlus

Printed and bound in Great Britain by
Clays Ltd, St Ives plc

About the monologues

Articles of Faith

Life decisions can take us down various possible paths, sometimes extremely different. This monologue, in two parts, explores one man, a vicar, faced with particular life experiences that could have turned him or strengthened him. The two parts are named ***His Wonders to Perform*** and ***Blaze of Glory.*** The monologue examines not only an individual's reaction to life experiences, but the testing of his religious belief and faith in a real world.

Splitting Hairs

A ladies' hairdresser makes discoveries about himself and his partner that lead to an unsettling climax. It examines strength and weakness of character, prejudice, integrity and self-interest.

Impure as the Driven

Maureen, married to a schoolteacher who she sees as driven by his total dedication to his school and his pupils, sees herself as a neglected wife. Her search for fulfilment leads her into deep waters. Just as it seems that she has found some answers, devastating events shatter the very foundations of her existence.

A Delicate Balance
(Pontius Pilate)

A new look at the Easter story from contemporary sources that shows Pontius Pilate as a man who is arguably a victim of his own background, struggling to cope with the situation outside his experience. The Easter story also becomes the tragedy of Pontius Pilate.

Dedication

To my friends in Mole Valley
Scriptwriters' Group and the WEA for
their help and and support during the
development of these monologues.

ARTICLES OF FAITH

Part 1

His Wonders to Perform

Words in Edgeways.

ARTICLES OF FAITH Part 1

HIS WONDERS TO PERFORM

(We find ourselves in the study of The Vicarage, somewhere in Surrey. The incumbent is Rev. Christopher March. It is dusk on a Thursday evening in the early autumn. The study is utilitarian but with a distinct feminine influence in the decor. The furniture is old well worn but practical. The wood though faded is well polished. There is a desk, bookcases, chest of drawers, two easy chairs and a stack of chairs for seating meetings. The desk is down stage right and has the only concession to the late twentieth century, a computer, ancient by computer standards but adequate for typing out sermons and general parish business. There are various family photos on the desk and around the room.)

Vicar *(entering the room as he calls to someone outside)*

It's sermon time I'm afraid, Janice, *(turning halfway back to the door)* but if I'm not out in an hour, dear, a black coffee wouldn't come amiss. *(Seeming to hear a reply, he smiles to himself and crosses to his desk with its word processor and sits down with a sigh of quiet resignation.)*

Ah well, Lord, here we go again. It is obviously as difficult for You as it is for me, otherwise I am quite certain I should feel more inspired. One would have thought after 25 years it would have got easier, not harder. Twenty-five years. I find that difficult to believe.

(He meditates a moment and a thought seems to strikes him) Now just one moment ... *(opening a drawer and rummaging through)* I do believe...Now lets see.... in here I think ... No

....In here *(trying another draw),* Yes ... I thought so. Here it is. And yes, I was right. Twenty-five years ago this coming Sunday. The very date. Would You believe it. The day I was ordained. Well, You should remember, Lord, You were there. Or, at least, I hope You were.

I suppose that means we ought to come up with something a bit special. Not that anyone here knows ... I hadn't married my darling Janice then. It was many years before I met her. So she wouldn't know the actual date. But You know and I know.

St Marks. That was the real start, wasn't it. Do You remember St Mark's, Lord? Oh Lord, that first sermon! Of course I'd done a lot of theory and had some practice at college. But as a curate at my first parish ...

My Vicar, 'ARTY' - everyone called him 'ARTY'- R.T. Short for Reverend Thomas they told me, but it wasn't. The R was his Christian name, Rawnsley. He never used it. It was the last vestige of Rawnsley Archibald Thomas. He'd even dropped the initial and signed most things A. Thomas. R.A.T is not the most desirable set of initial. One evening when we were chatting together he told me that the name Rawnsley meant 'One who lives by the raven's meadow'. As the parish was called Ravensmead I thought that it was his little joke, but I looked it up afterwards and I found it was true. Strange coincidence ...

Anyhow 'ARTY', in his wisdom, decided that it would be best to chuck me in the deep end and had me preach my first sermon in the parish the very first Sunday that I arrived there. I believe that I was more nervous that day than I was at my ordination. I don't know whether it showed or whether he just suspected my nervousness. He was a wise old bird, was

'ARTY'. Anyhow, you remember how he showed me the bottle of brandy that he kept hidden in the vestry. He said it was for his heart. He told me "You have a nip or two just before the service and you'll feel right as rain". And remember what happened, Lord?

I did as he said, but one nip didn't seem to have any effect at all, so I had a second. That seemed to help a little, so I had a third. Then I remembered that, even though it was only half an hour till the service, it would be a good hour or more before my sermon. I was afraid that its effects might wear off, so I had a fourth. That helped me throw all caution to the wind and had a few more. Do You remember that sermon, Lord? I believe it went down in the legends of St Marks.

'ARTY' was very good about it, mind you. He said it was all his fault. But I couldn't forgive myself. Not until our young curate, John Bean, did the same thing. I felt so much sympathy for him I found that I could finally forgive myself, too.

Now there's a topic for a sermon that I haven't used for a long while, 'Guilt and Forgiveness' in all its forms, highlighting self-forgiveness … as against self-justification that is. I don't think I should tell them the story of my first sermon though, do You Lord. There are too many who disapprove of my trips to the Green Dragon as it is.

If the Good Word is anything to go by, You weren't averse to a drop of wine Yourself. Quite the connoisseur, judging by the quality of the wine You produced for that Marriage at Cana.

You know, Lord, I sometimes think I'd have a far larger congregation if I held the services in the pub rather than the

Church. That would bring an outcry from certain sections of the congregation. I remember there was a vicar did that a few years ago when his church was badly damage, by fire or wind or something. He suffered major condemnation from some of his church community. The papers and T.V. picked up on it. When he was asked how he felt about his critics I remember he said, 'My congregation falls into two groups: those who glory in their religion and those who suffer it.' I know just what he meant.

(He gets up and crosses to draw the curtains over the French window)

Take our Mrs Christian, for example - I swear she married Mr Christian just to get his name. Anyone, who dedicates so much of their life to wallowing in condemnation of the sins and short comings of others, can't possibly understand love or the joy of forgiving. She never misses an opportunity to take me to task. I sometimes think I offend her code of conduct by just living.

Yes, Forgiveness could be a good topic, Lord ... for Mrs Christian and a few others that we both know.

What alternatives can I think of? You know my routine. For New Year I try to find a theme for the coming year. At the start of the month, an Idea for the Month, using general or topical subjects for the other Sundays. But a 25th anniversary ... Now that's a toughie.

Perhaps if I think back over the years ... Compared to some I suppose I've had it easy. No missionary work in wild, savage and heathen lands like Africa ... And ... and ... Brixton. Just

Cumbria, Buckinghamshire, Cornwall, and Surrey. Though they were a bit wild in Cornwall.

Remembering. *(pause)* Remembering. What great lessons have I learned in the last 25 years/ *(chuckles)* Funny the things that come to mind. That takes me back to school days, Ruddington College and Col. Foster-Green. He was my Housemaster. You and I weren't as close in those days, Lord, but I'm sure You remember. If a boy wanted to go down to the village or go somewhere special, he had to get a pass signed by his Housemaster. On Saturday, after lunch, those boys wanting passes would line up outside Foster-Green's study and he would sit there happily writing them. Suddenly and for no apparent reason, he would refuse to give a boy a pass. Not because the boy had been misbehaving in any way.

The boy would ask why. 'Because I said so' the Colonel would growl.

'But that's not fair, sir,' the boy would grumble.

'And a valuable lesson, too. Fair! Life isn't fair. Now get out.'

If you lacked confidence he would build you up but show overconfidence and he could reduce you to tears.

He believed he was breaking them in gently to the knocks in life. I couldn't have done it. But there was no malice in him. His motives were totally sincere.

It always seemed that he chose the victims at random. None of us knew if it would be our turn that week. On reflection, I could see there was nothing random about it. They were selected most carefully. A lesson in life.

He must have been gone nearly 20 years now. Yet I'm sure that we all remember the simple lessons he taught and found them to be true. I hope there are people in all my congregations who will be able to say as much of me, when I'm gone.

Jenny Carter died yesterday. But you'd know that, Lord. She lived for others until her final breath. Always that infectious laugh. Never laughing at other people though. Just at life. Despite the considerable pain she was in, she kept smiling until the last. Towards the end, whenever I went to visit her, I couldn't help wondering who was supposed to be cheering up whom? I always came away feeling strangely fortified. There are many people in the town who owe a great deal to Jenny. And I'm no exception. Look after her, Lord.

Understandably, Bill Bate is grief stricken. The two of them had been together for twenty years. Jenny had been a widow. Bill's wife had become so violently mentally ill that she had to be committed, and after all those years she still lives in a mental hospital. Bill would never divorce her.

As old friends, he and Jenny had decided to live together. 'Living in sin' as Mrs Christian was always quick to point out. Poor Mrs Christian, she will never understand the love that Jenny and Bill gave to the world, asking nothing in return, not even the love and respect that they earned. Keep an eye on old Bill too, Lord.

Thinking of Mrs Christian reminds me of the run-in I had with Mr Mortimer, another of our local zealots. I got into his bad books last Sunday. He cornered me after the morning service.

"Vicar!" he said, "do you think a man who plays the trumpet on Sunday will go to heaven?"

Remembering that his neighbour was just such a musician, I said, 'Well, Mr Mortimer, I can see no reason why a man who plays the trumpet on Sunday should not go to heaven, but I do have very grave doubts about the man who lives next door.".I know it was wicked of me Lord but the vision of Mr Mortimer in his seething self-righteousness was too much for me. I just couldn't resist it.

I must admit,though, that I'm not without some sympathy for Mr Mortimer. I remember ... now where was it? Oh yes, the vicarage at Lower Ashington. The old vicarage had been sold off just before we came. It had been vast, cold and impractical. The new one was a semi yet quite spacious and so much easier to maintain.

Our neighbour, Mr Fiddler, had one of those electric organs and he played it morning, noon and night. We were getting quite desperate. I remember, Lord, I even talked to You about it. Mind you, he was very good, but you can have too much of even a good thing. I could not think what to do. Vicars do not complain about their neighbours. Suddenly one night the answer came to me.

I was listening to a repeat of Dylan Thomas' "Under Milkwood" on the radio. Quite a favourite of mine. It got to those lines ' its organ, organ all the time with him' and Mrs Organ Morgan wife of the church organist says, 'I'm a martyr to music', and suddenly I had the answer. Miss Withers, our church organist was 82 and always asking me to find a replacement for her. We had a remarkably fine organ. I was sure that, given the chance to play it, Mr Fiddler, my neighbour, would enjoy it. I would then ask if he would like to take over the job of church organist. If he accepted, I knew it would ease our problems immensely. He would need to practise on the church organ; he couldn't play both at once and we would get some relief. It worked beyond my wildest dreams. He devoted all his spare time to the church organ and rarely played with his own. Or should I say on his own organ. I'm sure there is a lesson to be learnt there.

I think I'll put 'forgiveness' off for a while. But I won't forget it.

So, back to reflection and the years gone by. *(rising and crossing dl)* When I started out I was a bit of a fire-brand. It all seem so simple. I would just change the world. I couldn't understand why one of my predecessors or colleagues had not done it before me. I beat my head against that brick wall for many years. Then the disillusion set in. I saw all the suffering, pictures of starving, dying children with distended bellies. The innocent seemed to suffer and the bad to thrive. You know how I nearly gave it all up. Then I met my darling, Janice, *(crossing in front of desk, he picks up a picture of her)* she came to a service of mine and stopped to talk.

I remember that for the first time I spoke frankly of my doubts. Oh, the shame I felt and all the more so because it transpired that she had returned from missionary work in Africa. Illness had brought her home and she would not be allowed to go back. Bit by bit, she helped me rebuild my faith and remodelled my ideas. She showed me a real world where You Lord, worked through people. A world of so much sorrow that the simplest relief brought the greatest joy.

(Crosses to centre stage.) Yes, I think I feel a sermon coming on.

[BLACKOUT]

(Nearly a year later. We find him entering the study again)

Lord, don't the weeks fly.

Its nearly a year since Jenny Carter died. And within only a few days, Bill Bate's distressed wife, Mary ,died in her mental hospital. Whilst Jenny's death was a tragic loss to the world, in their own ways both deaths were a great release. Jenny freed of all her pain and Mary from both mental and physical imprisonment. Then only six weeks after that, Mrs Christian lost her husband. That was most unexpected. It was food poisoning. Mrs Christian was distraught. She saw it as her own fault. I then had this strange idea. I don't know what came over me. I'm sure you were behind it, Lord. I asked Bill if he would do me a great favour and call on Mrs Christian for me. I pointed out that although neither of us were her favourite people, I thought that their mutual tragedies might make him more easily acceptable to Mrs Christian than I would be. Bill thought it was a splendid idea, but then Bill would.

Now I reckon it was Bills doing and Bill says it was that sermon on forgiveness that I eventually got round to. Who knows? Mrs Christian seemed to undergo a conversion that would rate high on the scale of miracles. I'm sure that the conversion of Paul, or should I say Saul, of Tarsus caused no less wonder or joy.

Today I officiated at a wedding. Mrs Christian is now Mrs Bate. And I'll bet that Jenny Carter is laughing for all she's worth.

ARTICLES OF FAITH

Part 2

BLAZE OF GLORY
(or What might have been.)

Words in Edgeways.

ARTICLES OF FAITH Part 2
BLAZE OF GLORY

(At first glance the study seems to be the same but one become aware of subtle differences. There is no photo on the desk or anywhere else. The feminine touches are also missing. The whole room looks dull. The more so by contrast with the sunshine outside.)

Vicar. *(entering the room and going to his desk)* Oh God here we go again. Another damnable sermon, *(sits)* and it has to be a new one this week. People are starting to spot the old ones coming out again and again. Mrs Christian said last week "Vicar its getting quite like the television … all these repeats.' Thought it was quite witty for her. Malicious and funny. She really is surpassing herself.

Twenty five years of sermons. Preparing sermons is like preparing a meal with very limited ingredients. After 25 weeks I felt that I had exhausted all the alternatives. After 25 years, what can I possibly come up with that's new, how can I preach a sermon that will sound fresh and honest? I remember I got roaring drunk to preach my first sermon. I wish I could always be roaring drunk. It wouldn't hurt so much. The empty verbiage, fatuous clichés. I know the sermon I should preach had I the courage. It would go something like this.

(Rises)

My sermon today begins with a story that is very close to home. There is this father. He has many, many children. His children are allowed to squabble and fight amongst themselves, often with such a ferocity that they actually kill and maim each other. He watches but does nothing to intervene. Some of his children live in the height of luxury gorging on rich food and living a sumptuous lifestyle, while others of his children in another part of the same home die of starvation, in squalor.

Can you believe it? It is a true story. When did it happen, I hear you ask? It is happening now, this very day. He who calls himself a father. What father could behave like that? Will he be prosecuted and thrown into gaol for criminal neglect and abuse of his children? What will happen to him? I will tell you what will happen to him. We shall sing his praises every Sunday here in this Church. We shall kneel down and worship him.

Look on the starving of the world. Look on the carnage of the centuries. People fighting for the right. What right? The right religion. The right political ideals. The right to perpetuate an endless procession of hatred through the generations. Each conflict lighting a fuse to detonate the next war, rebellion or ethnic cleansing. Count the dead and know the truth and then decide where humanity should really place its faith and trust.

Yes, that's the sermon I really believe in, if I only had the courage to preach it. It would, of course, be my last sermon. I should be whisked away and the Church would presume to make my excuses. 'The poor man had a breakdown.' All very sad. And a new incumbent would arrive to perpetuate the lies.

What kind of man am I, who can proclaim aloud these lies as truth? And for what? Just a roof over my head and a measly stipend. A man who does not want to die alone in poverty with no pension and few friends. Disillusioned at 55 with no option open but to live a life without fulfilment, without honour.

Where in hell's name did it all start? I was full of such a

strength of faith and sense of purpose to begin with. Where did it all go? One thing is true. They compare entering the ministry to marriage. A very fair comparison. You fall in love. The blindness of love swamps you. You see nothing and feel everything. Eventually, the chemistry fails and you awake to the reality. It is very sensual and seductive, religion. It captures you in the highly scented rose garden of sweet smelling ideas and splendid vistas. But look close and you will see the roses are covered in blight and the smell is sickly sweet, whilst the splendid vistas are just painted on canvas. The promise of spring becoming the decay and rot of autumn.

I suppose the first seed of rot was sown early. School was my first experience of life's hidden falsehoods. In particular, that bastard, Foster-Green. Called himself Colonel, but the phoney was only a Lieutenant Colonel. He just lived to shatter our illusions. Build you up then smash you down. He was the only master who loved the beginning of term and hated the end of term. I think holidays meant that he had to live with himself and that was unbearable. He was a lonely and bitter old man who only found joy in breaking boys' hearts. But then I was resilient … then my spirit was not for breaking.

It was towards the end of school days that religion first hit me. I wanted to become a missionary. To tell the wonderful story to every living soul and inspire them with the joy and certainty that burned within me. It even stayed with me to university. It was only as ordination drew near that the first doubts crept in. I told myself that it was a big step that I was taking. Doubt was only natural. Just 'pre marriage nerves.'

Once I was working, everything would be wonderful. And while it was all new, it seemed wonderful. Then the glamour vanished. I saw a world - oh, such a world. A real world of the living, the suffering and the dying. A world where people who had lost their husbands, wives, children, turned to me for an explanation. That look in there eyes, when all I could offer were cliché, banal and empty platitudes learnt by rote ... That look burns my soul more than hellfire ever could.

I remember ... a young woman, Janice ... Something ... I can't remember her surname. She came and spoke to me after the service one Sunday. She came back to the Vicarage and we talked for quite a long while. For the first time I spoke frankly of my doubts. It transpired that she had been a missionary working in Africa. She spoke of the starving, the sick and the suffering with the same fervour I once possessed. But to me it was the same sick clichés I had always heard. She talked of finding joy in all this horror. I was devastated that such a beautiful and supposedly intelligent young woman could be so close to such brutality and remain so blind. I found her attractive and we met frequently and talked but finally unable to agree, we parted. Oh yes, the work she did with the sick and dying was highly commendable. I don't believe that I could have done it.

Perhaps I should dedicate a sermon to her. To Janice. But what to say? These days the news is full of the starving in Africa. Certainly God is going to do nothing about the situation, so a sermon about mankind doing God's job for him is near enough to the Orthodox theology to keep the congregation and the Bishop happy and almost honest enough to save me from more lying.

[BLACKOUT]

(Bring up lights)
Well it's done. I have just walked out of the church in the middle of the Sunday service, having preached that sermon that I have always wanted to preach. Today I finally found the

courage. It was short and to the point and just as I had always rehearsed it in my imagination. And on those final words 'Count the dead and know the truth and then decide where humanity should place its faith and trust', I stepped down from the pulpit and walked straight down the nave between the pews and out through the west door. I could have slipped out through the vestry but I had to see their faces. It's ironic, but the church has never been so full. No one moved. No one tried to stop me. They just sat there in stunned silence. I know that I made Mrs Christian's day . She's wanted to see the back of me for a long while. Hellfire and brimstone vicars are more her style. *(He picks up an envelope from the desk.)* My letter to the Bishop is written but I think I will read it through just once more before ... the next stage of my plan. *(He opens the envelope that is unsealed and takes out the letter.)*

Dear Bishop,

By the time you read this you are sure to have heard about my final sermon, so the rest will not come as a surprise. I could no longer go on living a lie. The creed of the Church and the articles of faith had become empty and meaningless to me. I could not believe in the Son of God when I did not believe in God. I see a world where we praise and worship this God, the Father Almighty, who, if he exists neglects his children totally to starvation and death, and yet we put a single parent mother in gaol for neglect of her children whose sin was merely to leave them alone so that she could go to work, to get money enough to feed and cloth them. How can we live with such contradictions? Such blatant inconsistency? Such obvious fallacies?

Once, I believed in the possibility of one united church. All I see is many, all of them split within and against each other.

Now, not only, my Lord Bishop, do I no longer believe in God or the church, I no longer believe in Mankind. There is no future for such as I but the path I have chosen to take.

I remain etc. etc. *(He replaces the letter in the envelope & seals it)*

(He places the letter on the mantelpiece)

I now see the real truth. I live in a world of insanity. All the world is mad, by degree. We cling to our religion, not because we believe in it but because it gives a pseudo richness to life. It helps us to face the horrors of life by showing us how to paint them a different colour. Pain and suffering are blessings that we share with the Son of God. Tell that to the hungry, the tortured, the raped women and children. How honoured those who suffer must be. This customized opiate, Religion, is designed to makes an ugly world seem beautiful. And like all drugs once surrendered to, it is addictive. Believers dare not let go for the reality is intolerable.

Through the ages, mankind has clung to his religion with the same fervour that a child clings to a favourite doll, fighting with hysterical passion. The birth of religion was like someone dropping a lighted match in the fireworks box. All very pretty but look at the damage it did.

Last night I awoke screaming from a nightmare, to find that the reality was a nightmare from which I could not awake. Would that I could learn again the trick of switching off the truth. But I have found a solution. Bill Bate supplied it. He didn't know, mind you.

Whilst I have always been able to dismiss the misguided lives of most of my flock with a laugh, Bill has always made me feel so bloody guilty. He and Jenny Carter seem to do all the good works and visiting of the sick that I should be doing. And doing it far better than I could ever do it.

Bill's wife has been in a mental institution for over 20 years. He'd looked after her till she became so violently insane that he had no alternative but to have her committed. Yet his faith remains unshaken. Jenny Carter was widowed within only a few years of marriage. She and Bill had been firm friends for some time, so after Jenny's husband died, they chose to live together. They did so much in the parish together it seemed only natural. The Mrs Christians of the parish frowned on it but I believe the rest looked more to Jenny and Bill than they ever did to me. The guilt, of course, came from within. It was never inflicted. They have both always been true friends to me. How much they suspected I shall never know. They showed no sign of condemnation like some others, and were the most frequent visitors to the vicarage.

About six months ago, Jenny became seriously ill. The pain grew quickly so that, eventually, even the strongest painkillers had little effect. Bill was desperate. Last Monday evening, he came to see me. He was haggard and exhausted. My heart dropped when I saw him at the door. The strong man of my parish was now turning to me, the broken reed for support. I could not imagine what there was that I could say that could give him any solace. But I had nothing to fear.

When I brought him in here he passed me a package and said, "I want you to take this and get rid of it for me. I cannot trust myself with it any longer."

I took the package from him. I opened it and stared at the contents in astonishment. Inside was a gun. It was a revolver, and with it the tools to clean it and a box of ammunition. The very thought of Bill Bate even owning a gun was so utterly alien to me that I stared at Bill in total disbelief. There had to be a logical explanation but ...

'It's not really mine' he said 'I have been off work for a few weeks to look after Jenny as you may know'

I didn't know. I should have made it my job to know. But I didn't.

Of course I said 'Yes'.

He went on, 'As Jenny slept a lot in the early days while the painkillers were still effective, it gave me time to do a lot of those jobs about the house that needed doing but that I had never found time for. One job I did was to turn out an old trunk that had been my fathers. The gun was at the very bottom of the trunk. Father must have brought back with him after the war.

'Later when Jenny first began screaming with the pain, the idea of putting her out of her torment kept creeping into my mind. To begin with, I had looked at her pillows and thought how easy it would be to just take a pillow and ...

'I know it's wrong and I know Jenny would believe it to be a sin. I believe that it's a sin. She might even fight to stop me. That would be intolerable. Then I would find my mind harping back to the gun. That could be done in an instant. She would know nothing and the sin would be totally mine ... not hers. Take it to the police. From time to time, the police declare an amnesty on firearms for people to hand in guns without fear of questions or prosecution. If I'd known I had it then I should have handed it in at the time. You on the other hand would be able pass it to them, tell them the truth without naming names.'

I told him to leave it with me. I would attend to it. I was relieved that I could actually do something for him. I asked him if he would join me with a coffee or something stronger, but he declined. He explained that he had left Jenny asleep, exhausted after a particularly violent bout of pain and he did not want her to wake up and find he was not there. He showed himself out.

The strange irony is that Jenny Carter did not wake up, but went into a coma and died that night.

(He reaches into a drawer and takes out the gun)

I sat staring at the gun after he'd gone. Thinking of Bill and Jenny. Then thinking of me. I picked up the gun. It felt strangely beautiful in my hands. Here was a reality that you could cling to. I could see no lies, no contradiction in it. It dealt in death. I examined it and found out how it worked. I loaded it. I was going to use it there and then. To die, to sleep. But to go out with a whimper was not for me. I had to do it with honesty and honour, stating what I truly believed.

(He gets up, still holding the gun.)

Well I've made my statement and, in doing so, I have cut the last cords that connect me with this life. Now those few friends I had will be so no more. At last the time is right. But not in here. I do not want to spoil this place. The garden is perfect. And look, the sun is shining. It's a lovely day for it. *(He exits to the garden carrying the gun and, after a few moments, a shot is heard)*

[ENDS]

SPLITTING HAIRS

Words in Edgeways.

SPLITTING HAIRS

(Jacques is 39. The set suggests part of a hairdressing salon. There are the usual special chairs, mirrors, basins, hairdryers, the general paraphernalia of the business, a reception desk and chair. Jacques, seated in one of the hairdressing chairs, is gently spot lit. He is facing the mirror. The rest of the area is unlit, suggesting the shop is closed. He swings round in the chair to face the audience as the spotlight comes up slightly.)

Funny ... but I actually considered becoming a priest at one time. I think I fell in love with the theatre of it. Being a hairdresser is not so dissimilar. Priests listen to confessions and, in our own way, so do we. Hairdressers I mean. But for us though, it's not just in the role of father confessor, but counsellor and therapist. We can't forgive 'em their sins, give them, what's it called, absolution, but I say a trouble shared is a trouble halved, and all at no extra charge. And if they've been pampered and left the salon confidently beautiful, it's a job well done. I'm sure absolution wouldn't make 'em feel any happier and it keeps 'em coming back to Maison Jacques.

Do I care about their problems? God no. Got quite enough of me own. But sounding like you care is good ... for business anyway. Remembering too is good – their names and what they've told us. And should your mind go blank, there's always those ambiguous little questions to fall back on.

My favourite when I've forgotten what me client said last time is something like, "Things sorting themselves out at home, Mrs Dwyer?", asked with sincerity and a knowing look at her reflection in the mirror. It works a dream. And if she doesn't remember either, it doesn't matter. She's bound to try to think what she might have said and that way you'll get the latest news anyway.

I'm the Jacques of Maison Jacques, by the way – to my customers that is. To my friends and family, I'm Jake. Living 50 miles away I can lead this sort of double life. Well, our ladies seem happy to share their confidences with us, my partner Piers and me, because they see us as safe. We learnt early on that in the hairdressing business, it pays to be gay. And our act, bitching like a couple of old queans, just helps to paint the picture and give them a bit of a cabaret. We work well together. It's a great partnership. And by partner of course, I mean business partner. I'm most definitely straight and pretty conventional – married with 2.8 children – the new baby is due in about six weeks. I can't speak for Piers though. Ours is a working partnership. Oh, I like him. Couldn't work with him if we didn't have some sort of rapport … quite impossible.

He has a charm and a grace that's, well, almost girl-like. You can't help but love him ... Like him, I mean. Everyone does. And as far as the rest of the staff go, he's almost one of the girls. But, mind you, we don't live in each other's pockets, and he's usually kept his private life to himself. Lives on his own now; I do know that. Used to live with his mother, till just recently. Met her several times. Very forceful woman, if you know what I mean. Was always in the salon nagging the poor boy about something. To her, Piers was still a five year old. It was a bit of an in-joke. If anyone spotted her coming in time they'd shout 'Mum Alert' and, if he wasn't with a customer, he'd beat a hasty retreat for the back office and out the door. Once she had gone, he'd creep back in. What it must have been like for him at home I can't imagine.

(pause)

They say that she fell down the stairs and broke her neck.

(pause)

I wouldn't suggest Piers doesn't seem upset. He does. Very. But not the way you'd expect. He's become very introvert, which is most unlike him. And jumpy – the slightest thing sets him off. And our merry backbiting cabaret's become uncomfortably real and unfunny. Even the customers have begun to notice the uneasy atmosphere. But he's insisted on working the last few weeks, right through the police inquiry and the coroner's hearing.

(Go to black)

(Come up on Jacques down stage centre.)

I shut up the shop today for the funeral and I went with him to offer my moral support. I was shocked to find it was just him, the vicar and myself, and of course the undertaker's men. I felt that was really rather sad. It was a burial, which is not that usual these days. Very austere but apparently it was what she wanted. It was very much in character.

Either the vicar had another appointment or he believed from Piers' strange indifference that the whole thing was an embarrassment to us, for it seemed to me that the ceremony was completed at an almost unseemly pace.

It had been drizzling a bit while we were in the church but it was stopping and the sun was breaking through as we reached the graveside. Piers had on a full-length black leather coat, slightly damp from the rain. It suited the day and heightened his pale, delicate complexion. There must have been a wedding before the funeral for an eddy of wind caught up some of the confetti from under a tree and proceeded to shower it over Piers where it stuck to the wet leather of his coat giving it a grotesque carnival look. He didn't seem to notice to begin with. He stood at the graveside utterly motionless, like an exotic black marble gravestone. He was not listening to the vicar and his thoughts seemed to be miles away with the fairies. Yes, I suppose, that is an unfortunate turn of phrase. He came to life again as he finally spotted the confetti. Removing it then became a priority - an obsession, but the dampness had made the specks of paper stick tenaciously and his efforts to remove them became even more frantic till, finally, he broke down into desperate, hysterical sobbing, interspersed with cries of 'Mother, how could you, how could you?' Like the confetti was in some way her fault. But I was unsure exactly what the sobbing was about. His mother's death? Maybe, but I don't think so. The confetti? Certainly it was a part of it. But I was fairly certain that there was something else. By then, the coffin had been lowered in to the ground and the graveside part of the service was over. The vicar, perhaps feeling guilty at his ill-judged haste became very much kinder and more conciliatory and helped me calm down the distraught Piers and guide him to a seat.

When we finally left the churchyard, I took Piers for a stiff drink in a neighbouring pub. I suggested that he might like to come and stay with us for a few days but he wouldn't accept. I drove him back to his home and I left him alone at the empty house with its ghosts.

(Go to black)

(Come up again on Jacque sitting at the reception desk.)

Thank goodness over the last six months since the funeral Piers has gradually got back to his old self. My wife ,Mary, gave us a gorgeous baby girl, Roberta, and Piers gave her a solid silver Christening mug and a beautiful ring that had been his mother's. He said it had been his mother's idea. That did quite surprise me.

It was good to have him back to normal. And the clients noticed. To be fair, he always had a better recall of his clients and their lives than I did and, with his recovery, this skill returned. As I always say, remembering your client's stories is important. And he was always discreet. Repeating what you've heard to others is an absolute no-no. Again just like the seal of the confessional. Only the other day Mrs B ... Oops I nearly said it. Let's say Mrs R let slip that she had a gentleman friend and it was all getting a bit steamy. Terrified that her husband might find out, she asked me for advice on how to break it off amicably. It was a quiet day and we were on our own in the salon, otherwise I don't think she would have been quite so frank – with Piers, perhaps, but not with me. I made the right noises so that she talked her self through it. Thanking me for my advice ...,hmm, what advice ... she left. It couldn't have been more than five – ten minutes later when in comes her best friend. She too was in a real state. Worried her husband was having an affair with someone. Nasty – very nasty. But you can't say a word. Things have to take their course.

Piers is the best of the two of us when it comes to the chat, but then he really cares and that's what makes him special. But then again, I'm the better hairdresser. Won several national competitions.

(Go to black)

(Come up on Jacques who is sitting on a chair centre stage.)

Things took a rather disturbing turn today. It was the first anniversary of the death of Piers' mum. I had wondered how he'd cope and trod very carefully. For the first part of the day he was on good form. I began to think that I was worrying about nothing. He was perhaps a little distracted so I knew that the date was not lost on him. I hardly expected that it would be. You would have to have known him as well as I do to spot the subtle difference. Maybe he worked a bit too hard at being cheerful. Seemed even keener to please. Then suddenly out of the corner of my eye I saw Piers staring at the door apparently frozen to the spot. I turned to look myself and saw that two policemen had come in. A credit card gang was working the town and they had come to warn us. I jotted down details and descriptions and the two police officers left. I glanced up at Piers again. He was as white as plaster of Paris. It seems the sight of the police had brought back the whole nightmare. Somehow he got through working on his client then he fled to the office. He sat out in there for about an hour. I kept popping in to see how he was and eventually, apologizing profusely, he returned to working but neither his mind nor his heart were in it. As we cleaned and shut up the salon at the end of the day, I suggested we might go for a drink. We hadn't been in a pub together since the day of the funeral. It was unusual at any time; Christmas with all the rest of the staff of course, or occasionally to discuss business matters and then usually with the solicitor or the accountant. Anyhow, he did agree to join me … seemed almost enthusiastic.

The pub was busy with the usual after-business drinking cronies probably trying hard not to go home. We found an empty table.

I could see that it was going to be hard work. He was very unsettled … sank his first drink in one go. I got him another. I tried to get him to talk about things but he wouldn't be drawn. He talked, mind you, nineteen to the dozen but about anything, rather than what was really troubling him. I also caught him staring at me in a strange, searching sort of way. He then rambled on about general inanities, client chat, high street gossip and every time I made a serious attempt to steer the conversation back he would make an excuse, once to buy drinks, then excusing himself to go to the loo on three occasions. It was in the other bar. Because of the frequency of the trips I actually asked him if he was feeling well and he just said there had been a long queue and he hadn't been prepared to wait. The drink seemed to be getting to him too, and far more than I would have expected. The last time that he returned from the loo it was via the bar and carrying more drinks. I suspected that he had been topping up in the other bar and going to the loo was an excuse. As I knew I would be driving, I had stuck to soft drinks after a first half of lager, but Piers had brought me back a double brandy and what looked like a triple for himself.

I said, 'Thanks Piers, old lad, but I really do have to be good, driving home, you know the score. You have it if you like but I'll get myself a soft drink,' and I made my way to the bar taking some of the empties with me.

As I stood waiting to order my drink, I could see Piers' reflection in the mirrored back of the bar. It's funny, people's mirrored images can look so different. I'd spotted it before in the mirrors at work. I then realized that this time it wasn't just the mirror. He was staring at me in a way that I'd never seen before. There was a strange intensity that I found most unsettling. As I turned to look directly at him, he switched his gaze to the tabletop as if it had suddenly become the focus of his life. I left the empties on the bar without buying a drink and returned to Piers.

'I think that we've both had enough, don't you? I'll take you home,' I said firmly.

To my surprise, Piers agreed without any argument. He lived quite near to the pub so I thought a walk home and the fresh night air would do him some good. The stroll to the house was completed in silence. I had never been into Piers' house before so when he invited me in, I agreed. Just idle curiosity, I suppose.

I made the coffee. I remember thinking that it was funny that I seemed to know instinctively where everything was. It was just where I would have expected it to be, I didn't have to ask once. We obviously thought alike. Soon our banter slipped comfortably into what we normally kept for the customers back in the shop. There was a happiness to it and somehow it suddenly seemed so natural.

"There you are, you old quean," I said as I handed him his coffee and sat beside him on the settee.

Slowly and deliberately, he put his coffee on the coffee table in front of us and took my left hand in both of his. I wanted to snatch it away but somehow I couldn't.

'I want to thank you for all you've done for me over the last year.'

'Don't be silly,' I said. 'It's not necessary.'

'No, you have been wonderful. I could not have got through it without you.'

'I was just doing what any friend would do.' Piers' grip on my hand was fierce now, as if his life depended on it.

'Oh no, you have been special'. I was about to argue and then ...

Then I saw the tears. Piers was crying. And some how those tears mattered. I placed my free right hand on top of both of his. I felt his painful grip relax to a great gentleness and the look in his eyes changed to one of intense need.

And that ... that was when we kissed.

Just to comfort him.

[Fade to black]

(Come up on Jacques who is standing behind the chair scentre stage.)

I had forgotten to ring Mary so the next day I was faced with explaining to her where I had been all night. She was cross that I hadn't rung but said that she understood my concern for Piers and that I had done the right thing to keep an eye on him.

I'd like to say that it didn't happen again, but it did. And to begin with, Mary put up with it. Then, one occasion as I arrived home about two o'clock in the morning, she said bitterly, 'You need to remember exactly who you're married to.'

That was two shocks in one night, for Piers had asked me to leave the family and come to live with him. That could never happen, and Mary and the children could never find out. She would never understand that there was nothing to it. Just a silly bit of self-indulgence to help Piers.

I decided to tell Piers that it had to stop. He was at first totally disbelieving, then distraught. He talked wildly. His declarations of love were desperate.

'I have loved you since the first time we met, but while mother was alive I could do nothing. I had to be free. And even after it was over, I had to wait to avoid arousing suspicion.'

Although I pretended not to notice those few words, in that instant I understood his real secret. The depth of his passion for me was suddenly clear. In the light of such a commitment of love, I knew what I had to do.

'I do understand, Piers, believe me. I can see just what it means to you, and me for that matter,' I said and kissed him lightly. 'But now I must go. I need time to think. But we will talk, perhaps on Monday, after work.'

That was Friday. If the weekend was a nightmare, working through Monday with the anticipation of what the evening would bring was worse.

The last customer gone, I went into the office with Piers. Seated comfortably on the settee that we kept in there, I talked about the rotten way his mother used to treat him. I persuaded him to open up about the events the night that his mother died. I said it would be therapeutic.

'I didn't often stand up for myself,' he said, 'It wasn't worth the grief but that night mother had been sniping from the moment that I arrived home and then something happened that turned it into a major row. It was about that long black leather coat of mine. I had just it bought that day and she saw it as a waste of money. She had just walked into my bedroom and seen me unpacking it. I said it would have been nice if she had knocked first.

' "I don't have to knock in my own house," she shouted.

' "Mother, I deserve some respect. I am 37. I am not a child."

' "That is a matter of opinion. An adult wouldn't waste money on a stupid coat like that," and she swept out. I was really angry and I ran after her. I caught up with her at her bedroom door. It is right at the top of the stairs.

' "Mother, the way you treat me is insulting."

'She turned towards me with her back to the stairs and slapped my face.'

'And that was when it happened?' I prompted.

'Almost. After the slap I stared back at her defiantly and she slapped me again. But with all her energy this time. I'd had enough. Years of suffering her scorn and abuse burst into a blazing white furry.'

'So it wasn't an accident?' I queried

'No, I pushed her. I pushed her as hard as I bloody well could. I couldn't take her manipulation, her belittling and bullying any longer. I had to be free. I just had to be free.'

'But murder?' I said sounding shocked.

'But I thought you understood. You said that you cared.'

'Cared for you in your loss, of course. But I can't condone murder.'

It was then that the police walked in. I had let them set up the hidden microphone in the office the night before. They had heard enough.

(He takes his bunch of keys out of his pocket, shakes them to get at the key he wants and starts to leave. Light follows him. As he nears the door, he stops and turns down stage)

As they took Piers away, he shouted back, 'You fucking coward.' I can't for the life of me think what he meant.

[BLACKOUT]

[END]

IMPURE AS THE DRIVEN

Words in Edgeways.

IMPURE AS THE DRIVEN

Scene: a sitting-room. Maureen is about 40. We find her dusting and tidying.

Oh yes, Martin's dedicated all right. As a loving wife, I'm sure I should admire it. He never stops. His pupils come first in all things. Perhaps if we'd had children of our own it might have been ... Hm! ... Perhaps!

(She sits)

Sometimes he spends whole nights at his room at the School House. Even during the school holidays he runs extra tuition from there. I'm sure Catherine, next door, sees more of her Alan and he's a long-distance lorry driver. And holidays ... we haven't been on holiday in 15 years. And when he does get home it's the computer. Can't imagine what he's up to but then I never could stand computers. Says it's research for his courses. The internet and the World Wide Web. It makes me think of spiders and they fill me with terror. Always have to get someone to get rid of them for me. I picture this humongous black spider as big as a hundred Millennium Domes, sitting in the centre of a web that wraps around the world, just grabbing people with its long tentacle legs and sucking them in, to poison them. I keep well away. *(she rises)*

(She picks up a large flower arrangement from a table.)

Mother says, "Why do you put up with it?" Then believe it or not, I find myself actually jumping to Martin's defence. Mother never liked him. "Too charming by far" she'd say.

Well of course I resent it … my mother telling me what to do at nearly 40. I could have bitten my tongue for confiding in her again. Every time I know what she's going to say and I keep on doing it. Just like I keep putting up with Martin.

(Carrying the flowers, she has crossed to the mirror above the fireplace.)

(addressing her image) Why do you keep punishing yourself like this?

(looking at his photo on the mantelpiece)

Oh yes he is very charming and good-looking. Everyone loves him. *(turning from the mirror)* They all tell me how lucky I am. He's the golden boy on the school staff. The Head likes him. The governors see him as suitable headmaster material, or so they told me. His colleagues love him and the pupils all love him, the girls in particular.

(Realizing that she still has the flowers, she bends to place the arrangement in the empty fireplace.)

When we were first married he was a wonderful lover. *(adjusts the flowers)* But that was then. He's always too tired now, if he ever actually gets home before I'm asleep. *(stands and steps back to admire the flowers)* I can't remember the last time we … *(her gaze falling on the deep shaggy pile hearthrug)* Oh yes, I can. It was last Christmas. We were on our own. His Mum and Dad live in New Zealand. Mine usually come for Christmas but last Christmas they had the flu and stayed at home. Actually Martin insisted, said, "I don't want them here spreading their bloody germs."

(She sits on the settee facing hearth and flowers.)

Martin got very drunk that night. The only light was from the Christmas tree and the flame flicker from the blazing log fire. Naked, and gently toasting ourselves in its heat, we made love on that very rug. For a while, it was like it used to be except for a certain drunken clumsiness and then, with passion spent, he fell asleep on top of me. For a while, clinging desperately to a belief that this was true love again, I lay there trying to think of him as an exhausted lover and not a drunken sod, when a large, red-hot ember exploded from the fire and landed on his bum. That woke him up, and I remember being astonished that someone so drunk could leap about with such agility.

He didn't like me laughing at him and somehow the more upset he became, the funnier it seemed and the more I laughed. I was nearly hysterical as he stormed out. Eventually, I went after him and tried to console him but he was much too hurt and angry.

(Go to black)

(Come up on her in the kitchen doing the washing up.)

I have decided to sign up for a creative writing class. It's at the local library, thank goodness; not at Martin's school like so many other evening courses. I wouldn't have gone if it had been at the school. With Martin rarely here, it seemed like a good idea and a super way to work out my frustrations. I don't think I'll tell him. He never listens to what I'm doing anyway, so why should I bother. I have to tell him most things two or three times before it sinks in and he's hardly likely to miss me. When he does come home and finds I'm out, I don't think he's that bothered. Usually when I've been out I get a perfunctory "So you're back". And if I do try to explain where

I've been, all I get in reply is a grunted "Whatever", without even lifting his eyes from what he's doing. I remember it used to be "whatever, dear" but recently the 'dear' has gone and sometimes nowadays it's just "Right" or an acknowledging "Uh huh". But then he never tells me about his day either.

I used to try to charm him round by playing the coquette but the only response that brought was, "For Heaven's sake, grow up woman". I once tried dressing in the St Trinians' look and he got really angry. He shouted, "What the hell are you suggesting," then almost screaming, "Get out of that rubbish now, and get rid of it". It was the closest he ever came to being violent. I remember thinking, 'Well, at least it's a response'.

When we entertain, which isn't often, I see a different man. The one he shows the world. The one everyone loves. The one I loved ... once.

We actually had a small dinner party last night. We had Jim Crowther, the head master, and his wife, Joyce, and Sir Henry Talbot-Wright, the chairman of the board of governors. Sir Henry is a widower but brought a partner with him, Avril. Very pretty girl. I understand she's 22 but I find that hard to believe. There are girls in the 6th form who look older than her. But then she reminded me so much of Grace Carter, a girl I was at school with. She always played young innocence ... with husband after husband. And they all had one thing in common. Substantial bank balances ... at least when she married them they did. Sir Henry is 72. I can't help wondering if he'll manage out live his bank balance.

She said to me, "It's true love, you know." We were here in the kitchen. It was after the main course and she had offered to help clear and fetch the sweet. She said, "People frown at the age difference but we're soul mates." Then as if she were sharing a secret confidence, she half whispered, "I believe in reincarnation, you know. Each time you die you come back as someone else. I believe that Henry and I have been lovers in several previous lives. Relationships like that are eternal, don't you think? Age gaps mean nothing, do they?" Noncommittally I said, "If that's what you believe." She said, "Oh it is."

Martin played the perfect host and I did my duty. He actually praised my cooking although it was only because Sir Henry did so first and as one of Martin's assets, he felt obliged to recognise me and add his own praise.

He said "Yes, good isn't it?" as he basked in my glory "Living with it, I'm so used to it, I forget". I cringed. Just for a moment I thought the 'it' was a reference to me and not my culinary skills. It replayed in my mind.
"Living with it, … I'm so used to it, … I forget."

It was my cooking he meant. I'm sure it was.

The Creative Writing classes start next Monday.

(go to black)

(Come up on her standing just inside open French windows, she has been gardening. She is carrying a single red rose.)

It must be nearly six weeks since I started at my Creative Writing group. They're a good crowd. Lots of would be poets. There's a fellow called John, a retired journalist who's working on a novel. Then there's Jean she's been a secretary and P.A. to some very senior executives in some "major PLCs", as she puts it. She's writing an autobiography. From what she's read to us so far, she certainly seems to have seen life. I can see trouble ahead there, if any publisher's brave enough to take it on. The tutor, Clive, is excellent. Makes us think about our work and other peoples. Doesn't allow it to become a mutual admiration society.

(She puts the red rose in a slender bud vase on the mantelpiece over the fire, removing Martin's photograph to make space.)

Then there's David, he writes plays. He is older than me by about 10 to 15 years, but he has a boyish charm that I find strangely unsettling. He always contrives to sit opposite me and catch my eye. After class today he stopped me in the corridor. He said, "Come for a drink." It was as much a statement as an invitation. I knew that I had to say no. Saying yes might give him the wrong idea. I always try to avoid making eye contact with him because when I do, something happens ... a warm quivering feeling that I know so well and scares me. I knew that that was a door that must never ever be opened; much, much too dangerous so of course I said ... "Yes I'd like that."

(Looking in the mirror; to herself)

Brazen hussy!

(turning away from the mirror, with a smile)

But it felt so good.

(Pause)

It was after midnight when I got back. Martin was still not home and I didn't care. It meant that I could save up my brilliantly contrive excuse for another time. Another time. Am I going to let there be another time?

(Go to black)

(Come up on Maureen sitting on a double bed.)

Playwright, David is actually a teacher. What is this with me and teachers? Not a colleague of Martin's, thank goodness. David teaches computer studies at another school. He says that I will need to learn to use the computer if I'm going to write seriously. I really don't fancy the idea but he said, "You need to move with the times. There is nothing to be scared of in computers." When he offered to teach me, I could hardly say no.

When I told Martin that I needed to be able to use the computer as I am taking evening classes, he said "Absolutely no way!" and, "I don't want you messing about on my computer, buggering it up". So later I said, "My teacher reckons he can get me a cheap one to start on". That did it. That evening, Martin came home with a brand new system with printers and everything. I certainly don't know much about these things but David was impressed when he saw it. He said, "I bet he didn't get much change from five grand". I must admit Martin has never seemed short of cash since his aunt died. That was when he bought this house. It's beautiful but five bedrooms for just the two of us … We never have people to stay except Mum and Dad at Christmas … It's a waste and the bedrooms still had to be furnished and still need cleaning. At least with the new computer, I can have a room to keep it in, so I don't have to look at it when it's not in use. Of course, Martin uses one of the rooms for his study but he keeps it firmly under lock and key. I think it's important that he has his own space. We all need that. Catherine, next door, was saying that, only the other day, when I told her. She said, "You've got your own space for writing and Martin has his". And while I'm amused by Martin's defensiveness, I'm not that interested. In fact, I've made a stand. I keep my room locked as well.

Martin's inheritance from his aunt has always been a bit of a mystery to me, and Martin was as non-communicative as ever. I never remember meeting her, I'm sure she wasn't on the wedding list and I don't remember a wedding present from her either. But she must have been fond of Martin to leave him everything. He has never told me exactly how much but it was most welcome. There always seems to be enough to buy whatever's needed and not many teachers can say that. A schoolmaster's salary doesn't allow for five bedroom houses and high living. Not that I get much high living.

Having said that, what with the writing group and my 'private' computer lessons, I am seeing a lot more of David. In the evenings, I go to his house a couple of times a week and, during the college holidays, he comes to me most days, if Martin's not here. My computer room still has a bed in it and a good strong lock.

I'm not writing as much as I should.

Go to black

(Come up on Maureen sitting at the kitchen table)

Had a bit of a shock today. I went to the doctor and he confirmed it. I'm pregnant. I've never bothered with contraception. Martin and I had tried for so long and he was so insistent it was my fault, I'd come to believe it myself. David always played it safe, but for once, when passion got the better of us. God, I was in a cold sweat when I left the doctor, but since I've got home and have had a bit of time to think about it and it doesn't seem nearly so bleak. Whilst in all likelihood David is the father, Martin doesn't know about David. Yes, he knows about David the computer teacher but not about David the playwright or David the lover. And David doesn't know about the baby.

I'm sure this is just what our marriage needs. A child of our own. To draw Martin's attention away from school and back to home.

What's more, about six weeks ago, something else happened. David had been away at a special course in Scotland for ten days. I was missing him like mad. Martin had come home early for once and seemed a bit low. I massaged his neck and shoulders. I'd never done it before. It was something else David had taught me. I had got the hang of it quite quickly. David said I was particularly good at it ... a 'natural', he said. Martin was certainly enjoying it. I had taken him completely by surprise. He said, "When did you learn to do that?" I could hardly tell him so I just said, "A friend taught me. It's nice to have someone to practise on". Martin could hardly know that I meant David when I said it. It's strange how I was learning to enjoy the deceit.

When I finally had Martin totally relaxed, I didn't give him a chance to say no. I jumped on him and, for once, he responded and we made love.
So the baby will be about three weeks early. These things happen.

I shall tell David that Martin has become suspicious that I might be having an affair and we need to cool it. As luck would have it the Creative Writing class moves to the school next term and David knows what I feel about that, so my not going will come as no surprise. Later I can tell him that

Martin's jealousy has revived our marriage and I'm pregnant. That should draw the final line.

I shall always love David. More for what he did than who he is. He brought such an intensity to my life and enabled me to break out of my prison. I know that prisons like that are only in your mind but David opened a hundred doors. Doors that can never be closed again. I'll always know who my baby's real father is. That will be my secret and my bit of David. A reminder to keep those doors open.

Go to black

(Come up on Maureen sitting in a simple room with barred windows and just a table and four chairs.)

About 5.30 this morning we were awoken by the most almighty crash from downstairs and voices shouting, "POLICE RAID stay where you are". Martin leapt out of bed and fumbled for his keys off the bedside table, dropped them cursed. He snatched them up from the floor and shot out the bedroom and off down the landing.

I pulled on a dressing gown and followed. I got onto the landing in time to see an incredible sight ... Martin actually struggling with two police officers at the door to his study. I remember feeling it had to be a nightmare – that I was going to wake up.

It was a nightmare alright but there was to be no waking up, at least not from sleep. I've spent the day in this room at a police station. Not our local one. I was questioned by one lot of officers after another about Martin, just questions after questions, mostly about Martin's movements but with no clue as to what it was about. I kept asking but they wouldn't say.

Then after I had been there about an hour, Marc Barnes, our solicitor, came in.

"Hello Maureen," he said very quietly and there was a level of sympathy in his voice that alarmed me. "Not good news I'm afraid. Martin is about to be charged on several counts along with other members of staff at the school." Nothing was making sense.

"Charged!" I said, "With what?"

Marc said, "The police have evidence that a child vice ring was being run from the school. Most of the staff have been taken in for questioning." He said, "And don't answer any questions unless I'm present."

I said "But surely Martin's not got nothing to do with it. He wouldn't get involved with anything like that."

"I'm sorry, Maureen, it looks like he might be. They have already found some pretty damning evidence on his computer and several of the children have come forward and made statements naming him."

"But it has to be a mistake," I said.

Marc said "I'll do the best I can for him, but it doesn't look too good"

"But not Martin. It couldn't be Martin". But already doubt was creeping in. The amount of time that Martin spent at the school, his sleepovers there, his attitude towards his computer, not wanting anyone to have anything to do with it.

It all seemed to fit. I wanted to remain loyal, but so much, that had happened, suddenly seemed to fall into place.

For a second I saw myself that night in the St Trinians costume and I remembered Martin's fury. I sat there with Martin gradually becoming a stranger in my head. I heard Marc's voice saying "Are you alright Maureen?" But I couldn't respond. To speak, there needed to be something to say, something that could be put into words but my head was full of mayhem. I was struggling in a maelstrom of emotions, with horror images flashing and swirling around my head faster than I could control them. I heard myself saying "No, No…" repeatedly but it wasn't a reply to Marc. I was trying to stop my racing thoughts, to shut myself off, but I couldn't.

The police doctor has just left. She gave me something and I have been told that someone has rung Mum and Dad to come and take me back to their place. But all I want is to hide away in my own home but they say that I'm not allowed to go there. Crime scene, isn't that what they call it? Crime scene! Do I really want to live in a crime scene. Suddenly nothing's safe, stable, reliable. And Mum'll love this. She will love this. All her suspicions vindicated.

Go to black

(Come up on Maureen sitting in a bedroom)

Mum has been wonderful. Not the slightest suggestion of 'I told you so'. I suspect that Dad's behind it. He doesn't often put his foot down, but when he does, Mum usually takes notice. He was always like that even when I was a child. I used to think he was a bit like Mr Bennet in Pride and Prejudice. He would let mother's furies and fancies wash over him or he would let me get away with a certain amount until he felt things needed calming down, then he would make his stand. Somehow it always came as a surprise, which is why he always got listened to.

The police say they've finished at the house but have advised me against moving back. Feelings are still running high and attacks on the house still happen. It's funny how that doesn't actually upset me. Somehow it was always Martin's house, never mine or ours. If the house went up in flames and I lost everything, in it I don't think I'd care. As I learnt about what had been going on, I was actually tempted to burn it down myself; an act of cleansing and breaking all connections with the past.

At least the bulk of the press have moved on to other things but the neighbours here still look at this house and whisper, and it is obvious that everyone regards me as guilty by association. It still never fails to make me feel dirty as if Martin's crime was an assault on me, too. His betrayal was a rape of my trust as much as any rape. And it would be much worse if I moved back to the house. Mum and Dad have put up with a lot, bless them.

Yet the sense of safety here in the old family home still isn't enough. I need David more than ever. There was the baby on the way and I needed to tell him that, after all, he was the father. I know he might be angry, if he feels I'd lied to him, but I was going to explain that I had got my dates wrong and there was no way it could be Martin's, which was of course true.

I've rung David several times, but he's never there. I leave messages but he's not rung back. More than anything I just need to talk to him now. Those things that I can never really talk about to Mum and Dad.

(Go to black)

(Come up on Maureen still in a bedroom.)

David rang back today. It was from a call box. He's agreed to meet me, but all a bit cloak-and-dagger.

When Martin was arrested, the judge refused bail, so Martin had been put on remand, along with the headmaster, most of the staff and the chairman of the board of governors, Sir Henry. They told me a day or two ago that Martin had asked to see me. Of course, I said no. How could he ask after what he had done to those children and what he had put me through?

(Go to black)

(Come up on bedroom.)

I finally got to meet David. We eventually finished up in London on a bench on the Victoria Embankment over looking the London Eye, David's idea, and I found out why. He was quite straight with me. He was sorry but in the light of the business with Martin, as a teacher himself, he could not be seen to be having any contact with me or my family.

How could he be that cruel after all we'd shared.

I felt utterly drained. I had seen David as the one light in my darkness, my escape back to normality. I was still carrying his baby and at, that moment, I vowed that he would never know it and that, for me, was revenge enough for his betrayal.

I've decided, after all, to go and see Martin. I realize that I need to. Martin, one of the 'Gang of Monsters' as the press named him, is the man I had married. I need to look into his eyes again, hear him speak again. There have to be clues that I've missed. Something in his eyes, in the way he spoke, in his body language. How was he able to fool me all these years? Marc, our solicitor, told me a lot more. He has dropped Martin's case. Marc's daughter was a pupil at the school. Sir Henry had been hand-picking staff, including the headmaster, to be sure they were all of one mind and no risk of fellow staff exposing them. The extent of the deception is unbelievable.

The irony was that it was actually Martin's actions that brought the law in. Not that he blew the whistle; far from it. It was his greed. Martin had been secretly filming much of the goings on and selling the videos on the internet. The police found some of the material on the internet and traced it back to Martin's computer.

Go to black

(Come up on Maureen still sitting at a dressing table.)

I went to the prison today. Martin was looking gaunt, which was hardly surprising. He had a black eye and a medical dressing on his cheek. He sat opposite me. I couldn't think how I had ever found him handsome. He said quietly, "Hello Maureen, thanks for coming," "Hello," I said. I couldn't bring myself to say his name. It would have been tantamount to giving some level of acceptance. He was looking at me intently, obviously searching for a hint that I might listen sympathetically. I said, "Well what do you want?"

He continued to look at me for a while, then finally he said, 'I just wanted you to know that I never laid a hand on any of the kids myself.' I said 'And you think that makes it alright. You were prostituting children and making money out of them'. He actually sounded exasperated as he said "For heaven's sake, Maureen, most of them would have been doing it behind the bike sheds whatever. Which was more risky, that or bringing it into a controlled environment and making them seriously rich into the bargain. Setting them up for life"

I can't believe he can talk ... to think like that. I said, 'These were children under your protection and you were using and violating them. You actually think the money makes it all right? You're beyond disgusting. You're inhuman' He actually went on, 'They were happy enough to take the money. Some were earning up to £5000.00 a night. We looked after the kids, made sure the money they earned was secure and that they came to no harm'. I screamed, "And you don't think what was happening to them was harm?" He didn't reply. The prison was heated but I was cold, so very cold. Suddenly, to me, he wasn't Martin any more. He was alien and he was no longer speaking a version of English that I could understand. I know that we had been slipping apart for years but this was different. This was nobody I knew or wanted to know. He watched me as I got up to walk away. I remembered his arrogance and it was still there in his eyes and as I turned and made for the door, I could feel those eyes on my back. I didn't want even his eyes touching me. I froze for a moment. I wanted to fly back to the table and tear those eyes out but, instead, I walked slowly out.

(Slow fade)

[ENDS]

A Delicate Balance

The Story of Easter through the eyes of Pontius Pilate

A Delicate Balance

Pontius Pilate
Not the easiest place to manage, Judaea. I'm a soldier and not a bloody politician. Born into the army, I was. Family tradition going back over three hundred years. Gaius Pontius, the great Samnite leader, is probably my most famous ancestor. Lead his tribe against a top Roman legion and, despite the odds, defeated them. We Samnites had a natural ability not to mention superior military organization. The remaining legionnaires were allowed to return to Rome, humiliated. Big mistake that – should have killed the lot of them. Rome learnt from its beating though, quickly adopted the Samnite methods, to return and take serious revenge. Over time, the tribes around Rome joined the Empire and Samnite soldiers are held in the highest esteem in the Roman army. I have fought all over the empire, mostly under Germanicus, yet, here in Judaea, I am in a civilian post with usually only a small militia of about 3000 local recruits to force the line. The region's true Roman legions are stationed in Syria, under the Legate of Syria's command.

So how do I find myself here? Now that's a good question. The one I most often ask myself. The simple answer is my wife. Whilst being stationed in Rome, I fell in love this girl and married her. Claudia brought with her, her family connections, a very mixed blessing. Claudia Procula was the daughter of Julia, the third wife of Tiberius, and therefore granddaughter of Augustus Caesar. That's some family connection. Yes, it brought with it certain advancement. It also moved me into unfamiliar territory: the plotting and scheming of the ruling families. I sometimes wonder if it is not a whole lot safer fighting on the frontline. Because the family saw my social status as well beneath that of Claudia, which is itself somewhat tarnished, when you remember that Claudia herself was illegitimate, I was a bit of an embarrassment to them, so I needed tucking out of the way. Which is why I'm in this godforsaken hole.

Of course, the legions were with me when I rode in to take up the post. Had to put on a show. Make it clear to the locals that I was in charge. My position is officially referred to as Prefect of Judaea. Some refer to me as the Governor of Judea and I don't put them right, but my 'humble' beginnings don't permit me the title, Governor. But the clout I lack in title, I make up for in brute force. There were one or two little uprisings but the ruthless application of the sword soon cuts things into shape. Only when they see their women and children being sliced up a bit does true terror instil order and obedience. It is my experience that the tougher you are, the less often you have to be tough. Cruel to be kind, they say don't they? If it were down to me I'd put the whole bloody lot to the sword. Problem over. Sadly, Rome doesn't see it that way, so the problems keep coming.

Unfortunately, I brought one of my biggest problems with me. The wife, Claudia. You see Tiberius was in fact very fond of Claudia, so when I was made Prefect of Judaea, my wife was, unusually, allowed to come with me, at my official request but at her instigation I hasten to add, not mine. In effect, I was ordered to make the request. There are times to make a stand and I was left in no doubt that this was not one of them.

They say men often marry wives like their own mothers. Claudia didn't have fiery red hair like mother has (and me too.), but she had the same fierce and passionate nature. Father had been in an expeditionary force sent to Caledonia, that's in the northern part of Britannica. My mother was a local tribeswoman. He took her originally as a slave but she soon changed all that and became his wife. I remember, when she told me the story, she said, 'Slave, wife, I can't really see the difference. I am still expected to answer his every whim.' She seriously loved him but talked to him like no other wife in the army would ever have dared. And I had to marry a wife like my mother.

I've seen my share of subversives come and go, but this man they call Jesus, I think he could be a serious problem. It was yesterday evening during the local festival they call Pesach, Passover, that I learnt that the Jewish religious leader their High Priest, Caiaphas wanted an audience with me, urgently.

I hate that word 'urgently' as it usually means trouble and any trouble out here needs nipping in the bud, so despite the late hour I agreed to see him. We have, if you like, a special relationship born out a sort of reluctant mutual respect. I hate his guts and I'm sure he hates mine but Caiaphas has almost absolute power over his people, and I wish that I had half his acumen as a political operator. He was in power when I arrived and has managed to survive all the upheavals. He presides over the chief priests and the Sanhedrin, the supreme council of Jews, which controls their civil and religious law. He's been High Priest for 18 years. Most High Priests survive about four years, which gives you some measure of the man.

Without ceremony he comes into my hall and from the door says clearly and quietly, 'Pontius Pilate, we have a problem.'

For the moment, I don't recognise this figure in a long black hooded cloak. Caiaphas is a slight man but he always dresses tall and gives the impression of dominance. The huge hood, his thick black beard and bushy black hair give the effect that his voice is coming from a black faceless hole. He removes the vast black hood to reveal his head with its extra tall head attire.

When I am uncertain what reaction is expected of me, I play bored. 'Come in Caiaphas and sit,' I say vaguely suggesting the couch to my left.

Caiaphas walks slowly to the couch and sits for a moment just looking at me. It is part of his technique for unsettling people. I'd been here before and was not going to fall victim to his mind games.

Finally I break the silence 'You say we have problems, Caiaphas. Spit it out. It's late and you are keeping me from my bed.'

'You honestly mean to say I have to tell you?' He says with the sarcasm of a father talking to a naughty child.

'You don't have to tell me I have problems. You and your lot are an endless source of those. Which specific problem do you have in mind?'
'Does the name Jesus mean anything to you?' the sarcastic tone as biting as before.

'Ah yes,' I say smiling, smugly I hope. 'The preacher. I imagine he must make you feel quite uncomfortable.'

'And you too, I should hope,' snapped Caiaphas. I'd certainly hit a nerve.

'The fact that this man is unsettling you is reward enough for me.' I was enjoying myself and his discomfort. I planned to milk it.

Caiaphas shakes his head. 'Did you not hear the news of his arrival in Jerusalem last week, through the Golden Gate what's more. Thousands lining the streets to greet him, shouting his name and throwing down palms before him.'

Smiling as sweetly as I can, I say, 'I can see how you might find that unsettling if the people begin to prefer him to you and your chief priests. But you have been in power for many years. Could it not be time for a change?' I suggest.

Struggling to bring his anger under control. Caiaphas responds quietly. 'If you cannot see how Jesus and his followers usurping power will upset the balance, then Rome sent the wrong man and perhaps I should write to Tiberius and draw his attention to it.'

Ouch, I believe he might do that too. My enjoyment wanes a bit. For various reasons I am not currently Rome's favourite son – yet another story – but I hope that I haven't shown Caiaphas any sign that he's unsettled me. Caiaphas, on the other hand, is too busy attempting to contain his fury. And I wasn't prepared to give any ground yet.

I asked, 'And you think I could help you how exactly?'

'The man has to be taken and put to death – crucified.'

'Ah so that's where I fit in. Only I can grant the death penalty. So you really do need me.' My moment to pause and stare at him. I enjoy his impatience, his agitation. Finally I say, 'Despite what you say I see no threat to Rome in this. I see no offence against Rome. Certainly nothing demanding the death penalty. Get him in, give him a good flogging and send him on his way'

Caiaphas leans towards me, 'If he continues to gain followers at the rate that he is, he will become a serious threat to Rome; you must see that.' Caiaphas is wagging his finger at me. The last person to wag a finger at me like that lost the finger.

'I must see it, must I? Caiaphas, my wife seems very keen on the man, never stops talking about him, and I have heard nothing from her to suggest any such a thing. In fact, quite the contrary.'

Caiaphas says, 'I am sure that Claudia Procula believes what she hears and hears what she wants to. But my spies tell me a very different story.'

'Ah your spies, of course,' I condescend. 'I believe your spy network is second only to that of Rome. But I am also sure that your spies tell you only what you want to hear.'

I am pleased with that but Caiaphas' response is quick.

'And when his followers believe that they are strong enough to overthrow the Roman occupation, and believe me they will, what then? He has already caused trouble in The Temple with violent behaviour. Surely it is better to take the heart from the group now, and quickly. Jerusalem is bursting at the seams with pilgrims for Pesach, over two million extra people. With this Jesus lighting the flame, all Jerusalem could be on fire before the end of the festival.'

Measuring my response to match I say 'I'll admit that that is an unsettling thought. But I think that you are being over-alarmist. Being Pesach we have many extra crack Roman legions here to keep law and order and prevent just such an eventuality.'

Caiaphas holds me in one of his stares. 'You know of course that he is claiming to be the new King of the Jews'.

I didn't, but I'm hardly going to admit it. And it makes a difference. A king is a figurehead for rebellion and Rome would not appreciate serious civil unrest under my watch. 'So what is your plan, Caiaphas?'

'I see that I finally have your ear.' The triumph in his voice is unmistakable. 'We are ready to make an immediate arrest tonight followed by an instant trial, so we can get quick approval of the Sanhedrin for the guilty verdict. And there is another reason for haste. On religious grounds he must be dead and the body taken down before Pesach Sabbath. And we dare not wait till afterwards. We cannot let this thing linger on. It would be much too dangerous. It has to be quick and clean.'

I can now see the way that this is going. Caiaphas is greasing the wheels, setting things in place and I say, 'Which is why you want to be sure that when you bring him before me, my approval will be forthcoming.'

Caiaphas smiles weakly and says, 'Exactly.'

'Caiaphas, you are as slick an operator as ever.'

Caiaphas rises. 'Can I then count on that approval when we bring him before you, tomorrow?'

Reluctantly I say, 'Based on what you have told me, I see no problems.'

Caiaphas thanks me and makes a hasty exit, saying that he is sure that I would understand his need to rush off. I believe, having the Jewish leadership on side makes my position stronger.

(Go to black)

INT *Their Bedroom*

Claudia is awake when I rejoin her.

She asks, 'What was all that about?'

Sitting on the bed and trying to sound casual, I say 'Just Caiaphas.'

Sleepily she grumbles 'At this time of night! What was so important it couldn't wait till morning?'

'It seems that this man Jesus is a subversive,' I tell her.

Suddenly, wide awake, she springs up and says angrily 'What rubbish! I've heard him preach, you know I have, and he preaches nothing but peace. He says to love your enemies, do good to people who hate you, if someone strikes you on the face, offer him the other cheek to strike. He has a large following of people who recognize his love of his fellow man and love him in return. Husband, does this sound like a man trying to overthrow the state? To me, I see a real asset to Rome – a man that you could work with to help keep the peace.'

I am thinking, if he really is the man that Claudia believes him to be, then indeed he would be a gift to the Roman Empire. If he, with his teaching, could persuade all the occupied peoples to become submissive to the Empire there would be no stopping us. I laugh out loud, not so much at Claudia's, naivety as at myself for even considering such idiocy.

I say, 'Sounds much too good to be true, and that's because it is. I'm sure Caiaphas wouldn't share your views. If staying in this godforsaken hole has taught me one thing, it is keeping Caiaphas on side that really helps keep the peace, and Caiaphas wants Jesus dead. He believes the numbers of Jesus' followers are growing so rapidly that the man represents a serious threat'

Claudia takes my arm as she says, 'It strikes me that it's Caiaphas who sees his own position threatened. His reason for wanting Jesus dead is his own self-interest. Thank goodness he can do nothing without your permission.'

'My dear Claudia, Caiaphas has made a good case for being really worried.'

'And you believed him?' Claudia asks.

'I listened to him,' I say noncommittally.

Claudia is looking at me in disbelief. 'Surely you are not saying that you actually agreed with him?'

'He gave me a lot to think about,' I hedge.

Claudia is now roused. 'Well I'll give you something to think about, something that I have not told you before, and something you have obviously not noticed.' I suspect that there is some sort of confession coming.

More quietly, she continues,'I put off telling you because I knew it would anger you. With my own eyes I have seen Jesus heal people.'

'It is never a good idea to mix with locals,' I scold. 'You know my feelings about that.' But I sense that there is more to come.

She hesitates, then it comes out in a rush 'Three days ago, I took Pilo to Jesus and begged him to heal Pilo's crippled foot.'

I can't believe what I'm hearing. She knows this breaks all the rules.

I shout, furious, 'You actually took our son to this man? How could you have been so damnably stupid?'

She shouts back "I did and he healed him."

'Rubbish!' I yell. Oh the stupid, stupid woman.

With accusation in her eyes, she says, 'You have been so busy, when did you last see your son?'
I try to remember. I say, 'I don't know'… This morning I think. I saw him playing this morning.' It's a blatant lie.

'And was he limping?'

'I can't say I noticed. But he has become good at hiding it. He is growing tough like a soldier.'

'He isn't limping because his foot is straight again,' Claudia exclaims. 'Jesus performed a miracle.'

'Miracles! There's no such thing.' I shout. 'You're getting simple-minded.'

She faces me out. 'I have now seen it with our own son as I have with hundreds of others.'

'And it's all clever trickery,' I protest, 'and it is just that, that makes the man so bloody dangerous.'

'Are you saying that you are giving Caiaphas what he wants?' she asks incredulous.

There's no point in lying. Quietly I admit, 'Yes, I have given him my agreement.'

Claudia goes mad and flies at me. I have never seen her like this before. She is hysterical. There is no talking to her. I hold her tight until she exhausts herself, then I lay her sobbing onto the bed as I leave the room.

I see little chance of getting any more sleep. That stupid cow! Here was a complication that I could well do without.

I decide to go to Pilo's room. The first thing that I see as I enter is his foot, sticking out from the bedclothes as if to answer me. There is no strapping on it. The foot is perfect. I can see no sign of the damage. There is no such thing as a miracle, I remind myself. Pilo stirs and I wonder if in fact I had said it out loud. Silently I keep on saying it to myself, like a mantra.

It was the exercises, it must have been. The exercises must have put the foot right. A doctor had had Pilo on a regime of exercises to correct the foot. Everyone knows the story about the terrible childhood accident when his foot went under a chariot wheel. The foot was saved but not from the crushing distortion of the bones and the terrible scarring.

Who am I kidding? It was a story alright and yes, that was of course exactly what his foot looked like, a crushing accident, so that's what we have always claimed. It was a convenient cover-up for weakness. He was born with the deformity.

Deformity is a sign of weakness, whereas an adventurous child having an accident is about strength.

For a moment I believe that I have remembered wrongly, so I pull back the bedclothes to reveal the other foot. The other perfect foot. A matching perfect pair. I stare. Looking for something. Not a trace of blemish.

But miracles … what rubbish. I try to remember the last time I saw his foot. You live with these things. If you don't expect change, you don't look. In fact, you try not to look. You just accept. The foot must have healed through natural causes. probably brought about through the binding and the exercises. It couldn't be anything else. He's grown out of it. It has to be that.

Pilo stirs in his sleep, then wakes.

'Father, is that you?'

'Go back to sleep, Pilo.'

'Why are you here?'

'Your mother mentioned something about your foot getting better.'

'Yes, Father isn't it wonderful. The preacher Jesus made it good again.'

I can't think what to say so I say nothing and turn to go. As I leave the room I know that I must hold to my beliefs. I must put Claudia and the child's suggestibility behind me. Weakness now would make my position impossible.

To-day the chief priests and a large rowdy horde have brought the man, Jesus, to me. Caiaphas has obviously won over the Sanhedrin. They have waited outside as their religion does not allow them to enter. The filthy scum say it would be unclean to enter. Yes, their entry would make the palace unclean, perhaps. The man Jesus is brought in under an escort of my soldiers.

As he is marched in, I see his once, perhaps white, clothing is bloodstained and filthy. His captors have obviously given him a tough time already. My soldiers are no more gentle and as they push him towards me, his legs entangle in his torn robe and he falls heavily at my feet. Something makes me step forward to help him up. I withdraw my hand at the last moment, shocked at my action. Jesus is already struggling to his feet. I just watch. He is standing and staring at me. It is not a pleading look, not an impudent stare, nor is it the challenging stare of the rebel. Somehow I feel naked before him. I feel certain that by some means he knows my innermost thoughts. And yet I sense no condemnation. I struggle to clear my head of these ludicrous ideas. If a man, so severely battered and beaten as he has been, can still emanate such a powerful presence it is not surprising he has so large a following. I remind myself that this, of course, is what makes him so dangerous. I am feeling a need to avoid his eyes, so I walk around him looking at the floor. I find myself grateful that he does not turn or follow me with his eyes.

The second time I pass behind him I say 'You seem to have made some serious enemies'. I get no response.

I continue to circle him. 'They consider that their case against you is strong.' No response.

I walk behind him again. 'They say that you threatened to destroy their temple. How do you respond to that?' He remains silent.

'Should I take your silence as an admission of guilt?' The man says nothing.

'They claim you say that you are the Son of their God. Not so shocking to me. Certain Emperors in Rome have been known to declare themselves to be gods. A bit delusional, even arrogant but not regarded as a crime. Are you claiming to be a god, too?'

He is so still, so silent, that if he were not standing I might believe him dead already. For my next question I face him. Face those eyes.

'Did you stir up the people against Caesar as they claim? That would be more serious.' I watch his face carefully. Not a flicker except possibly pity. Pity for me. I do not need his bloody pity. It is as if he is talking in my head. Without saying a word he is getting to me.

'Are you the King of the Jews?' I ask.

To this he just says, 'These are your words and the words of others who seek no true answer. I come to bear witness to the truth.'

I say 'What is the truth?' He makes no reply.

'Then answer me one more question, Jesus. Where are you from?'

'Galilee.'

At last I see a possible way through. Galilee is under Herod's jurisdiction. Herod, son of Herod the Great, is directly responsible to Rome, as I am. He may be a Jewish king but he is Rome's man. Herod, like millions of devout Jews, is in Jerusalem for Pesach. By passing responsibility to Herod, he, rather than I, will pass the death sentence.

Taking Jesus back to the people, I say, 'This man is a Galilean and is therefore Herod's responsibility. Take him to Herod.' The people are angry but take Jesus to Herod, much to my relief. I am advised that it is no secret that Herod would see him dead. He will, I am sure, view this as a favour, which could help our future relations.

The relief is short lived. Within an hour they return with Jesus. Herod, it seems, was just happy to mock and humiliate the helpless pretender and pass him back to me.

I return to the crowd. The crowd is very restless now. I look to the Chief Priests and ask 'What accusation do you bring against this man?' The chief priests, believing that Caiaphas has already obtained my agreement, are not well pleased.

Their response is blunt. 'If this man were not an evil-doer, we should not have brought him to you.'

I return, amid furious shouting, to Jesus. I find him standing patiently, facing my empty seat. I take the seat and ask again, 'Are you the King of the Jews?'

He remains silent.

This man is affecting me. I say almost pleading. 'You are

facing certain death. I cannot understand why you say nothing in your defence.'

Just then one of Claudia's servants brings me a message from her. Not surprisingly she was troubled with nightmares about Jesus and is demanding that 'I have nothing to do with this innocent man'. The servant who herself seems deeply distressed, also lets slip that not only Claudia but all her staff have become followers of this man. I feel my anger rising. This is a level of disloyalty bordering on betrayal. Lessons have to be learnt.

The man has to die if only to teach Claudia a lesson not to meddle with the locals. That way, when I tell her, she will be bound to blame herself for his downfall. A sound lesson I hope, to put her in her place and keep her there. But I still need to watch for possible repercussions. Surely he has to die to prevent insurrection. But if you learn one thing working for Rome, it's that your actions have the habit of twisting like snakes to bite you.

I return to the crowd. 'I find no case against this man but I see you will have it no other way.' Then I remembering the Jewish tradition of releasing a prisoner at Pesach and I announce 'As is your tradition at this festival I will release to you a prisoner. I offer you Jesus or Jesus Barabbas.'

The high priests have surrounded themselves with a well trained crowd who shout loud enough to drown out any counter calls, 'Barabbas! Barabbas! Release Jesus Barabbas' over and over again. As the shouting dies down I ask 'And Jesus of Galilee, what of him?' and the call comes back loud and clear, 'Crucify him! Crucify him!'

I call for Jesus to be brought out. I send a servant for a bowl of water. By the time Jesus stands beside me the tumult has receded slightly.

I shout above the crowd, 'I see that you will have it no other way.' I ask for the bowl, 'But I wash my hands of this man's blood. Take him and do as you will.'

Traditionally, a sign is set atop the cross of the condemned man declaring his crime. To please myself and perhaps Herod, I have ordered the sign to say "Jesus of Nazareth, King of the Jews" in Latin, Greek and Hebrew. Caiaphas and the Sanhedrin are incensed but I insist in having my way, and this gives me immense satisfaction.

It seems that Claudia and her servants have gone to the crucifixions. She blames me and says that Rome will, too. Why can't that woman leave well alone? Will she never learn?

A strange darkness has gathered over the whole area. I've seen nothing like it before. It has lasted for about three hours. It was as dark as night. The lamps all had to be lit. One of my advisers declared it to be an eclipse of the sun by the moon but another pointed out that Pesach is always set by the full moon and that it is impossible for an eclipse when the moon is full. As it ended, the ground shook violently, causing much damage; I thought that the palace was going to collapse. We all ran outside into the dark streets. News of all manner of strange events are being reported to me ever since. They say that the veil of the Temple has been ripped in two. Even the soldiers returning seem chastened by the wonders and events that accompanied Jesus' death. Claudia says that Jesus died at the same moment that the darkness ended and the earth shook.

A respected councillor, one Joseph of Arimathea calls on me to beg for the body of Jesus. He has his own private tomb. I don't hesitate but I feel obliged to make sure the operation is overseen by soldiers and that the grave is put under guard. I want no problems with the remains being tampered with. There is no telling where that could lead.

It's only three days since the crucifixion and there is more trouble. I have just been told that the body of Jesus has gone missing from the tomb. The guards who must have let it happen were from the local militia. They have been put to death for their negligence. The Jews are blaming us, saying that we removed the body to prevent it becoming an object of focus for an uprising. There are rumours circulating that Jesus' followers are claiming that he has risen from death. They claim, apparently, that he promised he would. This is my worst fear realised. We certainly didn't remove the body. It would be easy enough to disprove the rising from the dead if we had. And I fear that the same applies to Caiaphas and his crowd. Neither of us needs this. Ever since the crucifixion, Caiaphas' spies have been keeping a close eye on Jesus' followers and my spies have been keeping an eye on them, so it's unlikely that his disciples went off with the body. I really didn't need this. If this blows up as I fear it will, who is Rome going to blame? But what more could I have done?

It's his eyes. When I sleep, in my dreams, or when I'm awake, if I let my mind wander just for a moment, all I see is Jesus' eyes; I think that those eyes will haunt me for ever. In the name of all the gods, what have we been party to?

(Slow fade to black)
[ENDS]

Sources and notes

The King James Bible

The New English Bible

Who Moved the Stone by Frank Morison (Albert Henry Ross), first published 1930 by Faber & Faber Ltd

The Gospel according to Claudia and other internet references.

There are historical references that imply Claudia was the illegitimate daughter of Julia, Augustus Caesar's only natural offspring. During her first two marriages, Julia had several lovers and upon the death of her second husband, she married Tiberius. Julia's scandalous behaviour and lifestyle continued, causing such distress to her father, Augustus, that it resulted in her banishment from Rome and Tiberius divorcing her. While in exile, she gave birth to Claudia and shortly thereafter died. With Tiberius becoming Emperor, he found favour in Claudia and adopted her as his own daughter.

Claudia's letter was translated from an ancient Latin Manuscript first found in a monastery in Bruges, Belgium, where it had lain for centuries and is now referenced within the Vatican Archives. In recent years, the letter has been carbon dated and seems to date with some accuracy to the right period. Whilst this is no guarantee of authenticity, it has such a ring of humanity and truth to make it very interesting.

In the late 1920s Catherine Van Dyke, a literary scholar and the daughter of a prominent Detroit family, had rewritten Claudia's Letter into the English language under the title 'A Letter from Pontius Pilate's Wife'.

So this monologue should not be treated as gospel but perhaps as a very human interpretation of what might have been.

NOTES

Frank Morison's book is fascinating from many angles. Primarily it was the author's intention to write a book to show how ridiculous the story of the crucifixion and resurrection of Christ was. Almost miraculously that was not the book that was finally written. Morison was a very thorough historian and researcher and, as he gathered his data, he soon realised the true significance of the evidence that he found. He examines the subject not only from the historical evidence, but also argues a very sound psychological case. It has been claimed that the book has brought about numerous conversions to Christianity.

According to the Claudian 'Gospel' it seems that Rome blamed Pilate for his handling of the events of the first Easter and his attempts to stifle early Christianity, which is why he and his wife finished up with a farm in Gaul were Claudia exchanged letters with friends and it is these letters that tell the story of what happened.

The internet is also full of a lot more source material, most of which I referred to at some time when compiling this work. But essentially I tried to put myself into Pontius Pilate's shoes, a man with little knowledge of politics who relied almost totally on his experience, his harsh military life, and the other unsettling relationships with Roman aristocracy of which he had no experience before his marriage and plainly was not comfortable with. It is arguable that he was the wrong man in the wrong place at the wrong time and that his story is one of tragedy rather than villainy.